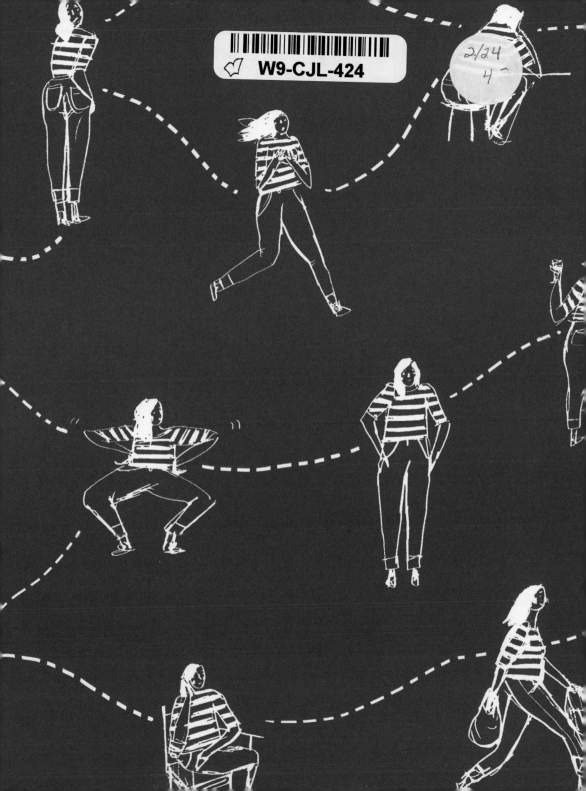

MY NAME IS GIRL

AN ILLUSTRATED GUIDE TO THE FEMALE MIND

by Nina Cosford

quadrille

MY NAME IS GIRL

by Nina Cosford

AN ILLUSTRATED GUIDE TO THE FEMALE MIND

Publishing Director: Sarah Lavelle
Creative Director: Helen Lewis
Junior Commissioning Editor: Romilly Morgan
Illustrator: Nina Cosford
Design: Claire Rochford
Production: Vincent Smith, Steve McCabe

First published in 2016 by
Quadrille Publishing
Pentagon House
52–54 Southwark Street
London SE1 1UN
www.quadrille.co.uk
www.quadrille.com

Quadrille is an imprint of Hardie Grant
www.hardiegrant.com.au

Text © 2016 Nina Cosford
Illustration © 2016 Nina Cosford
Layout © 2016 Quadrille Publishing

Cataloguing in Publication Data: a catalogue
record for this book is available from the
British Library.

UK ISBN: 978 184949 800 5
US ISBN: 978 184949 840 1
Printed in China

CONTENTS

INTROD

MY NAME IS GIRL* AND THIS IS
MY LIFE. MY UPS AND DOWNS AND MY
SOMEWHERE-IN-THE-MIDDLES, TRYING
TO MAKE IT THROUGH THE EVERYDAY
THE BEST (AND SOMETIMES WORST) I CAN.

JOIN ME ON MY DAILY STRUGGLES AS
I TEETER ON THE FINE LINE BETWEEN
BEING A GIRL AND A WOMAN, WHILST
TRYING TO FIGURE OUT WHO THE HELL I
AM IN THE PROCESS. FROM OBSERVING
WHO I AM ON THE SURFACE TO EXPLORING
THE DIFFERENT TYPES OF GIRLS I COULD
BE, TO ENTERING A CRASH COURSE ON
HOW TO BE A BETTER GIRL; THIS IS MY
ANGLE ON THE ASSAULT COURSE OF
LIFE AS A GIRL.

* ONE OF MANY

UCTION

YOU CAN COME WITH ME IF YOU WANT,
BUT BEWARE – THERE ARE SOME GNARLY
THINGS BACKSTAGE...

ULTIMATELY, GROWING UP IS ABOUT
LEARNING THAT I'M NOT (QUITE) THE
PERSON I ALWAYS WISHED I'D BE.
I'D SAY I'M MORE A WORK IN PROGRESS;
AN UNFINISHED DRAWING OR A HALF-WRITTEN
SONG I CAN KIND OF HUM BUT DON'T
HAVE THE WORDS FOR YET.

NOTE: THIS IS NOT A BOOK OF ANSWERS;
MERELY ONE OF QUESTIONS.

YOU ARE NOW ENTERING MY GIRL BRAIN...

CHAPTER 1

On the surface

EVERYTHING WE DO GIVES OFF AN IMPRESSION OF WHO WE ARE, OR MORE IMPORTANTLY WHO WE WANT TO BE. IT'S NOT ALWAYS FAIR TO JUDGE A [GIRL] BY [HER] COVER, BUT (LET'S BE BRUTALLY HONEST) WHERE ELSE WOULD WE START?

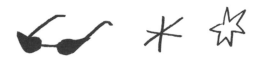

I'M AWAKE.

NOW WHAT? ...

ME
BEFORE
MAKE-UP

ME
AFTER
MAKE-UP

BUT WHAT TO
DO WITH THE

ELEGANT
WAVES

DISCO

PLAYING
IT SAFE

PERM

INNOCENT
PLAITS

SUPER
STRAIGHT

SASSY BOB

FUTURISTIC
BOB

WET-LOOK
CURLS

THE HIGH BUN

CLASSIC
BOWL CUT

SCHOOLBOY CROP

MICRO-FRINGE

RED DRESS

BROWN LEATHER BELT

CLASSIC JEANS

SPORTS BRA

CROPPED CARDIGAN

SKI SOCKS

WHAT TO WEAR?

BROGUES

BRETON TOP

KIMONO

BLACK VEST

HIGH-WAISTED VINTAGE SHORTS

CHELSEA BOOTS

BLACK TIGHTS

LBD

CRISP
WHITE
SHIRT

MEN'S
T-SHIRT

FAITHFUL BLACK BRA

DENIM
DUNGAREES

PLEATED
SKIRT

GRANNY PANTIES

FRESH WHITE
SNEAKERS

BLACK
POLO-NECK

WHAT'S IN MY BAG?

STALE GUM

MYSTERIOUS BUTTON

COMPACT BRUSH + MIRROR

STOLEN PEN

SQUASHED BANANA
THAT I'M TOO SCARED TO TOUCH

GRITTY LIPSTICK

FRONT DOOR KEY *

SCUZZY HAIRBAND

ILLEGIBLE PHONE NUMBER

* WHY DO I STILL NOT HAVE A KEYRING FOR THIS

EMERGENCY
TISSUES

STUPID
LITTLE
PENCIL

ASSORTMENT
OF PAINKILLERS

PLASTIC
JEWELLERY

ZIT CREAM

LONELY GLOVE

TAMPON

MASCARA

ELUSIVE
HAIR GRIPS

REDUNDANT
RECEIPTS

GROSS
FLUFFBALL

MY OUTFIT FOR
WORK

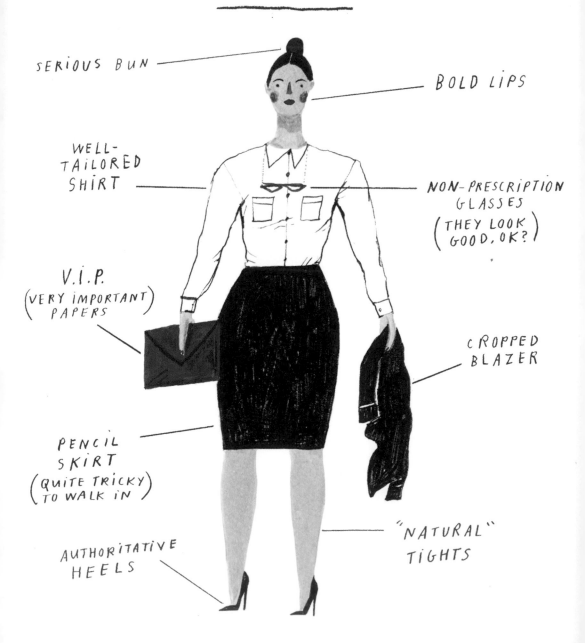

SERIOUS BUN

BOLD LIPS

WELL-
TAILORED
SHIRT

NON-PRESCRIPTION
GLASSES
(THEY LOOK)
GOOD, OK?

V.I.P.
(VERY IMPORTANT)
PAPERS

CROPPED
BLAZER

PENCIL
SKIRT
(QUITE TRICKY)
TO WALK IN

"NATURAL"
TIGHTS

AUTHORITATIVE
HEELS

MY OUTFIT FOR A
"COOL" PARTY

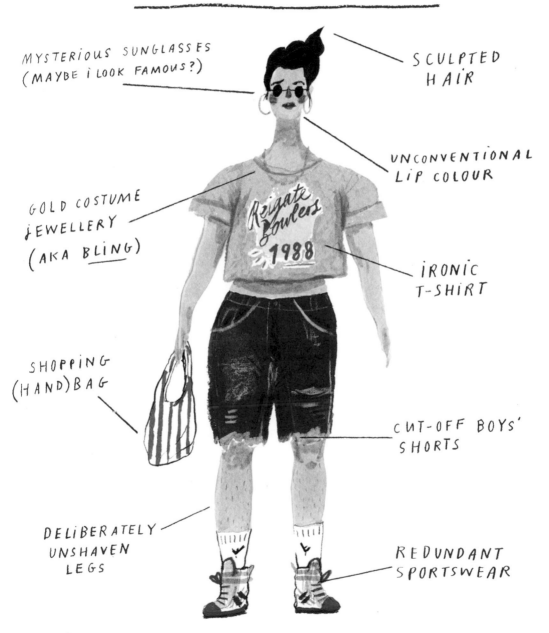

MYSTERIOUS SUNGLASSES
(MAYBE I LOOK FAMOUS?)

SCULPTED HAIR

UNCONVENTIONAL LIP COLOUR

GOLD COSTUME JEWELLERY (AKA BLING)

IRONIC T-SHIRT

SHOPPING (HAND)BAG

CUT-OFF BOYS' SHORTS

DELIBERATELY UNSHAVEN LEGS

REDUNDANT SPORTSWEAR

MY OUTFIT FOR TRAVEL

SUNHAT

NO TIME FOR MAKE-UP

UNWASHED HAIR

RAINCOAT

BRETON TOP

FILM CAMERA (KEEPING IT OLD SCHOOL)

MAP

BACK-UP CAMERA / COMPASS / MAP / PHONE / COMPANION

SCRUFFY "MOM" JEANS

WOOLLY SOCKS + HIKING BOOTS

MY OUTFIT FOR A
DATE

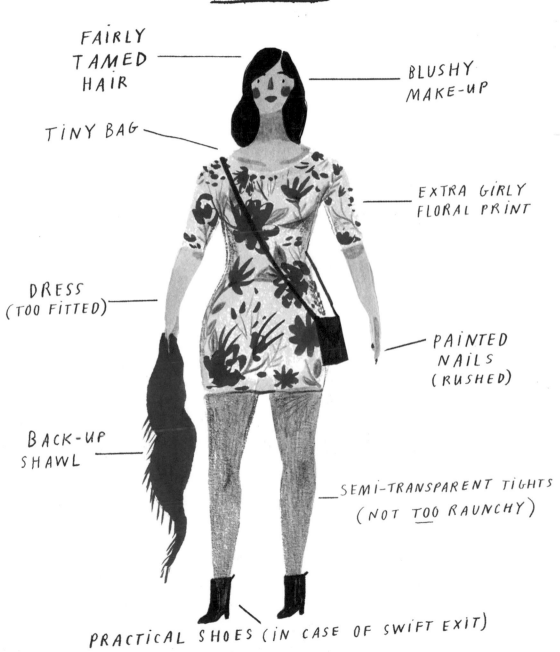

FAIRLY
TAMED
HAIR

BLUSHY
MAKE-UP

TINY BAG

EXTRA GIRLY
FLORAL PRINT

DRESS
(TOO FITTED)

PAINTED
NAILS
(RUSHED)

BACK-UP
SHAWL

SEMI-TRANSPARENT TIGHTS
(NOT TOO RAUNCHY)

PRACTICAL SHOES (IN CASE OF SWIFT EXIT)

THE DREADED NIGHT OUT

THE NIGHT OUT-FIT

A BIT OVERKILL?

Ballgown

Tiny dress

RESTRICTED LEG MOVEMENT

Dancing Queen Boots

SEXY/SCARY?

Leather Jacket

Belt/skirt

Playsuit

DESIGNED FOR GOOD DANCEABILITY

practical Handbag

Hotpants

Bralet

DE-SEXIFIES ANY OUTFIT

Cardigan

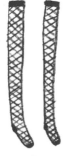

STRONG PROBABILITY OF BUTT REVEAL

BUT CAN I RUN FOR THE LAST TRAIN?

Fishnets

GIRL'S NIGHT OUT

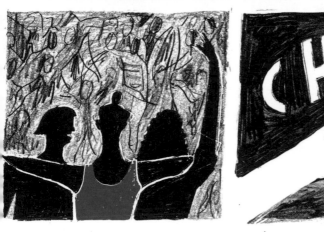

CHAPTER 2

Which girl to be?

THERE ARE SO MANY GIRL-DENTITIES OUT THERE TO CHOOSE FROM, i STRUGGLE TO BE ONE OF THEM THROUGHOUT THE DAY (LET ALONE LIFE). AM i ALL OF THEM? AM i NONE OF THEM? iF i DON'T DECIDE, WILL i BECOME NO ONE—OR WORSE—EVERYONE??

E	A	O	F	S	V	H	Y	X	P	L	O	R	B	Q	U	G	W	R
L	R	I	G	Y	A	L	P	N	K	M	Z	L	A	K	N	L	Q	F
J	H	E	A	R	T	B	R	E	A	K	E	R	M	P	F	P	M	N
F	I	T	E	M	O	C	A	N	O	V	Q	B	J	R	A	K	M	O
V	G	M	O	M	L	O	X	L	P	O	D	L	J	U	S	I	H	R
H	I	D	V	M	X	I	R	T	A	N	I	M	O	D	H	G	L	E
A	P	D	I	V	B	B	W	C	U	G	V	A	I	E	I	G	A	T
Q	U	N	P	C	A	O	Y	P	Y	I	O	T	L	R	O	L	M	S
T	X	R	O	O	L	B	Y	S	D	S	R	H	R	Z	N	R	I	U
D	T	W	O	S	L	D	F	E	Q	S	P	O	I	C	I	F	N	B
R	S	V	X	E	S	R	O	H	K	R	A	D	G	Y	S	O	A	L
A	I	Y	I	G	A	E	D	H	O	R	J	I	Y	N	T	R	Y	L
M	N	E	R	D	I	V	H	M	W	E	D	K	B	N	A	E	T	A
A	I	Z	A	Y	I	C	Q	H	A	K	N	Y	A	A	E	L	R	B
Q	M	O	H	B	D	U	O	V	I	A	X	E	B	F	Q	I	A	P
U	E	S	F	O	E	A	Z	E	O	M	A	Z	E	D	C	O	F	F
E	F	T	S	E	A	I	L	A	D	E	T	T	E	U	R	B	S	A
E	B	V	N	O	O	H	A	U	W	L	F	N	F	Y	Q	Y	T	V
N	O	X	G	Z	B	V	D	V	O	B	U	M	N	U	T	N	Y	I
W	O	Z	D	Y	H	L	I	I	G	U	Y	N	D	E	K	N	K	D
U	B	C	T	O	R	F	R	D	V	O	A	R	I	A	A	U	K	O
Y	Z	C	E	E	U	V	I	I	M	R	A	E	V	E	O	B	T	N
D	H	Y	O	T	G	V	D	V	G	T	R	U	Y	A	H	I	O	W
G	F	H	B	A	D	Q	X	E	R	D	M	I	C	N	Y	O	A	H

FIND YOURSELF

BABYGIRL ☐   TOMBOY ☐
MINX ☐   QUEEN ☐
DARK HORSE ☐   BITCH ☐
FASHIONISTA ☐   MOM ☐
DIVA ☐   TROUBLEMAKER ☐
PLAYGIRL ☐   NERD ☐
PROM QUEEN ☐   GIRLBOSS ☐
HEARTBREAKER ☐   PARTY ANIMAL ☐
BALL BUSTER ☐   LADETTE ☐
PRUDE ☐   BUNNY BOILER ☐
DRAMA QUEEN ☐   LADY ☐
DOMINATRIX ☐   FEMINIST ☐
GRANNY ☐   GIRL ☑

WHICH ONE AM i?

PART ONE

THE EASY GO-ER

THE THINKER

THE PLAYER

THE STIRRER

THE DREAMER

THE ADVENTURER

THE DOMINATOR

THE DO-GOODER

WHICH ONE AM I?

PART TWO

THE NURTURER

LA PASSIONISTA

THE REBEL

THE PRINCESS

THE
TWO-FACE

THE
CHAMELEON

THE
CENTRE
OF THE
UNIVERSE

THE
ANALYST

HOW TO TELL A GIRL BY HER SHOES

THE GOOD GIRLFRIEND

THE CHIC CHICK

THE LADY OF THE MANOR

THE LAZY LASS

THE ATHLETE

THE NEVER-GREW-UP GIRL

THE
ACADEMIC

SPRING
BREAKER

THE CASUAL
GIRL

THE DIVA

FEMME FATALE

THE
MOUNTAINESS

I WANT TO BE

THE ARTISTIC ICON

i WANT TO BE

THE
ELEGANT
LADY

i
WANT
TO BE

THE
FREEDOM
FiGHTER

I WANT TO BE

THE POETIC INTROVERT

GiRLS in t

THE
TIME-KEEPER

THE
COFFEE-MAKER

THE DEADLINE-CHASER

e WORKPLACE

THE ENIGMA

THE
EAGER PLEASER

THE BALL-BUSTER

WHICH ONE AM i?

LAUNDRY
NINJA

SENSITIVE
SUPERSTAR

THE BEST
OF ME

EXPERT
LISTENER

AWARD-
WINNING
GOSSIPER

JEWELLERY
UN-TANGLER
CONSULTANT

SELFIE
SPECIALIST

HOOVER
CHAMPION

HAIR-BRUSHER
EXTRAORDINAIRE

TEA-MAKING
MEDALLIST

QUEEN OF
LIST-MAKING

PROFESSIONAL
FRIEND

THE WORST/OF ME

OVER-analytical

HYPER SENSITIVE

1ST

PARANOID

High MAINTENANCE

mountain OUT OF A molehill MAKER

JUDGEMENTAL

SELF CONSCIOUS

FRETFUL

THE NAG-OMETER
How naggy are you?

THE ULTIMATE NAG — YOU WERE BORN TO NAG. YOU ALMOST THRIVE ON IT, AND NO MATTER HOW MANY TIMES YOU MIGHT APOLOGISE FOR IT, YOU ALWAYS FEEL YOU ARE JUSTIFIED TO NAG.

NAG PRO — NAGGING COMES RATHER NATURALLY TO YOU. IT CERTAINLY DOESN'T DEFINE YOU BUT IT'S A NOTICEABLE TRAIT.

NAG — YOUR WEEK ISN'T QUITE COMPLETE WITHOUT A LITTLE NAG AT SOMEONE. THINGS JUST FEEL A LITTLE MORE RIGHT WHEN YOU'VE DONE SO.

PART-TIME NAG — YOU MERELY DABBLE IN THE ART OF NAGGERY. WHEN YOU DO HOWEVER, IT IS OFTEN NECESSARY AND ONLY PRACTISED IN EXTREME CIRCUMSTANCES.

NEVER NAG — YOU COULDN'T NAG PROPERLY IF YOUR LIFE DEPENDED ON IT; IT JUST FEELS ALL KINDS OF WRONG!

CHAPTER 3

Beneath the surface

THERE'S ONLY SO
FAR YOU CAN CRUISE
THROUGH YOUR ROSE-TINTED
LIFE BEFORE YOUR INNER
GIRL BRAIN TAKES HOLD.
WE'RE ALL THINKING IT,
WE'RE ALL FEELING IT BUT
WE'RE NOT ALWAYS TALKING
ABOUT IT. ENOUGH OF THE
HIDING! IT'S TIME TO
DIG A LITTLE DEEPER...
ENJOY THE [BUMPY] RIDE.

NO FILTER

THE SHIT-TINTED GLASSES

I'M TIRED, UNSETTLED AND SUPER-SENSITIVE.
TODAY I'M WEARING THE SHIT-TINTED GLASSES...

YOU KNOW THAT FEELING WHEN THE WORLD LOOKS
LIKE AN UGLY BROWN MESS AND YOU JUST
WANT TO RUN AWAY AND HIDE?

I'VE GOT AN ANTENNA TUNED INTO EVERY
SHIT AND SAD FREQUENCY OUT THERE,
AND I HAVEN'T GOT THE STRENGTH TO TUNE OUT.

IT'S SHIT.

MY ENERGY'S LOW WHICH TOTALLY EXPOSES
ME TO OTHER SHIT. IT CLINGS TO ME AND
SUCKS MY SOUL LIKE A SHITTY LITTLE LEECH.

THE ONLY THING IS, THESE GLASSES ARE A GREAT FIT...

...SHIT!!

MY BODY HANG-UPS

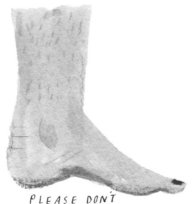

PLEASE DON'T
LOOK AT MY FEET

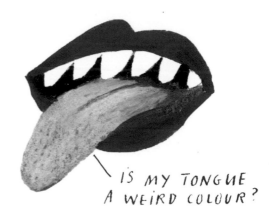

IS MY TONGUE
A WEIRD COLOUR?

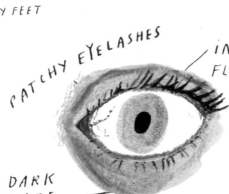

PATCHY EYELASHES

INCREASINGLY
FLABBY EYELIDS

THESE DARK
SHADOWS ARE
GETTING BAD...

MONKEY
EARS

WHAT IS THE
ACTUAL FUNCTION
OF EARLOBES
AND WHY ARE
MINE SO BIG?

FLAPPY ARM WINGS

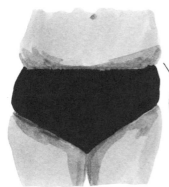

UNWANTED
OVERSPILL

ODD-SHAPED
LIMBS

EARLY SIGNS OF
NOSTRIL HAIR...
(BUT IT HURTS SO MUCH
TO PLUCK!!)

MILLIONS
OF
BLACKHEADS

ARE MY BOOBS
TOO LOW
FOR MY AGE?

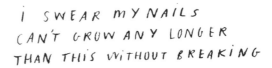

I SWEAR MY NAILS
CAN'T GROW ANY LONGER
THAN THIS WITHOUT BREAKING

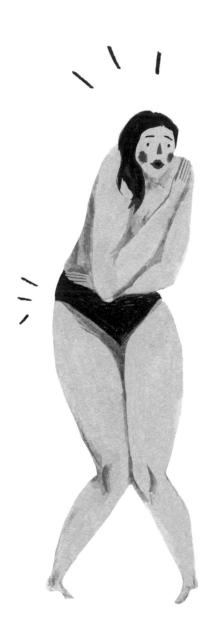

CHOOSING A BRA...

ANNOYING EMBELLISHMENTS

A bit too carnival queen?

WAAAYY TOO GIRLY

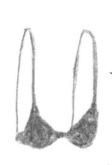

THIS CAN'T BE THE SHORTEST THESE STRAPS GO?!

POINTLESS BOW

wrong colour

This would just look tragic on me

SERIOUS RISK OF SPILLAGE

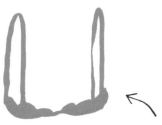

BUT WHERE ARE THE BOOBS MEANT TO GO?

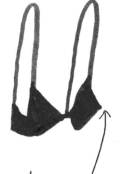

too pointy !!!

TOO BORING

i FEEL LIKE I'M HAVING AN AFFAIR IN THIS

These straps feel like dental floss

(For all those sports I do)

Dangerously comfortable...

WHAT'S THIS HOLE FOR?

Can anyone actually wear these?

The Contradictions of being a Girl

* **CAN WE JUST TALK ABOUT THIS?**

  SHUT UP AND LISTEN TO ME

* **CAN'T YOU JUST GIVE ME A HUG?**

  GET OFF ME

* **WHY DON'T YOU EVER SHOW ANY EMOTION?**

  GOD YOU'RE UGLY WHEN YOU CRY...

* **WHATEVER HAPPENED TO CHIVALRY?**

  DON'T PATRONISE ME YOU CHAUVINISTIC PIG!

* **I DON'T NEED YOUR HELP**

  ... BUT THIS IS PRETTY HEAVY...

* **NOOO! THAT'S VERY KIND OF YOU TO SAY**

  DID I TELL YOU TO STOP?

* **WHAT DO YOU THINK?**

  I'M NOT CHANGING MY MIND BY THE WAY...

i WOKE UP LIKE THiS

*PERFECTION IN A MATTER OF MOMENTS

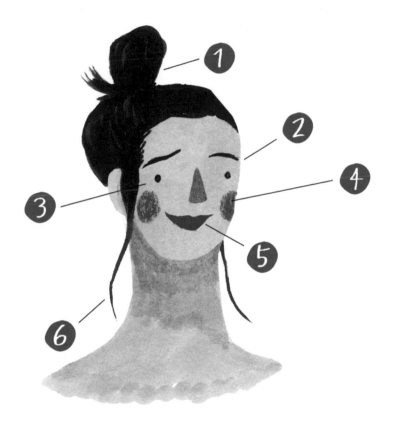

1. THE "MESSY" BUN
= 20 MINUTES

2. PLUCKING EYEBROWS
= 9 MINUTES

3. NATURAL-LOOKING MASCARA
= 4 MINUTES

4. PRIMER, FOUNDATION, BLUSHER
= 15 MINUTES

5. "NATURAL" LIP TINT
(WITH LINER UNDERNEATH)
= 2 MINUTES

6. "FALLEN LOOSE" STRANDS
= 30 SECONDS

MOODSWINGS

DON'T COME NEAR ME
DON'T TRY TO CALM ME
DOWN. DON'T TOUCH ME
JUST-LET-ME-BE
MAD !!!

ANGRY

EEEEEEEEE
EEEEEE EEE
EEEE EEEEE
EEEE EEEE
EEEEE EEEEE !!

EXCITED

Anxious

Those same old worries creeping
up on me especially at night
when I'm alone with my brain.
symptoms include the eye-twitch,
the hand-wobbles and the
notorious outbreak of skin-itch...

ROUNDABOUTS

Sad

I SHOULDN'T BE SAD. I'VE GOT NOTHING GOOD ENOUGH TO BE SAD ABOUT. THIS MAKES ME MORE SAD. EVERYTHING IS HEAVY AND THE WHOLE WORLD IS SAYING GO BACK TO BED.

Reflective

Sometimes it's good to step off life's relentless treadmill and take time to process the good and the bad in the past and present.

SULKY

DELIBERATELY CASTING A SHADOW ALL AROUND ME. i MIGHT WANT SOME ATTENTION! i MIGHT NOT! SO WHAT?!

ZEN

ALL POSITIVE. ALL DAY.*

* DON'T YOU DARE RUIN THIS.

A BUILD-UP OF
EMOTIONS CAN
ONLY LEAD TO
ONE THING...

THE CRY-AGRAM

7 SIGNS SHE'S ABOUT TO CRY

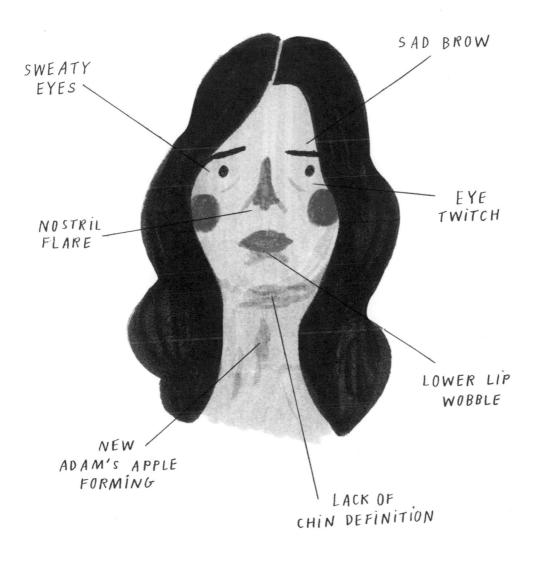

SWEATY EYES

SAD BROW

EYE TWITCH

NOSTRIL FLARE

LOWER LIP WOBBLE

NEW ADAM'S APPLE FORMING

LACK OF CHIN DEFINITION

OFF MILK
(ALREADY POURED)
ON CEREAL

UNUSABLE
HAIR GRIPS

**SOGGY
SOCKS**

BLISTERS
(AND NOT A PLASTER IN SIGHT)

PEOPLE WHO CONSTANTLY
MENTION THEIR AGE
(AND THEREFORE "WISDOM")

THINGS I HATE

PEOPLE WHO PUT
CANDY WRAPPERS
BACK

CRUMBS
IN THE BED

THE SOUND OF OTHER
PEOPLE EATING

**HAIRY
COMBS**

SMELLY WASHING-UP
SPONGE

HYGIENE CRIMES

UNFLUSHED

UNREPLACED TOILET ROLL

TOENAIL CLIPPINGS

LIMESCALE

LID AND SEAT UP

VARIOUS PILLAGES

PLUGHOLE OF HAIRS

ME SCENE DO NOT CROSS CRIME SCENE DO NOT CROS-

ABANDONED (WET) TOWEL

CRIME SCENE

SCATTERED PUBES

RIME SCENE DO NOT CROSS

GRIME

MY WORST

ω NAKED IN PUBLIC

i SUDDENLY FIND MYSELF WITH NO CLOTHES ON AND NO ONE IS WILLING TO HELP ME. THERE'S ALWAYS A MAIN ROAD THAT i HAVE TO WALK DOWN WHILST EVERYONE STARES AT MY BUM AND BOOBS.

⏰ RUNNING LATE

i KNOW i HAVE SOMEWHERE VERY IMPORTANT TO BE BUT i MISS A TRAIN, SLEEP THROUGH MY ALARM OR AM TRYING TO RUN IN HEAVY SHOES, GETTING NOWHERE.

👶 HAVING A BABY

A BABY APPEARS OUT OF NOWHERE AND i'M TOLD iT'S MY CHILD (DESPITE NEVER NOTICING THE PREGNANCY OR BIRTH). i'M SUDDENLY RESPONSIBLE FOR THiS TiNY FRAGILE HUMAN AND i'M ALONE WITH NO MONEY AND A MASSIVE SENSE OF GUiLT. SOMETIMES THE BABY IS A PUPPY BUT MOSTLY iT'S HUMAN.

NIGHTMARES

🦷 LOSING TEETH

ANYTHING FROM A SINGLE WOBBLY TOOTH
TO MY ENTIRE MOUTH CAVING IN ON ITSELF.

🚽 HELL TOILET

THIS DREAM SEEMS SO REAL I'M SURPRISED I DON'T VOM IN MY
SLEEP. I'M DESPERATE FOR THE LOO AND WANDERING ROUND A TOILET
BLOCK IN A GYM OR SCHOOL — ORANGE TILES AND NO WINDOWS.
WHEN I FINALLY FIND A VACANT CUBICLE (THAT ISN'T IN AN UNBEARABLE
STATE) I REALISE THE DOOR AND WALLS ARE TINY AND EVERYONE
IS PEERING IN AT ME SAT ON THE TOILET !!!!!!

🌊 TIDAL WAVES

A GINORMOUS WAVE APPEARS WITHOUT WARNING AND
SWALLOWS EVERYTHING AND EVERYONE IN ITS PATH.

CHAPTER 4

How to be a girl

I'M NOT GONNA LIE AND SAY BEING A GIRL IS EASY. IT'S NOT ALWAYS FAIR, IT'S NOT ALWAYS RIGHT AND IT'S CERTAINLY NOT ALWAYS RATIONAL. FOR BETTER OR FOR WORSE, HERE ARE SOME OF THE (IM)PRACTICAL STEPS WE HAVE TO TAKE THROUGH THE COURSE THAT IS GIRLHOOD.

THE FEMALE

THE EVERYDAY CHALLENGE.

RUNNING WITH BOOBS

QUESTIONS ABOUT THE FUTURE

UMM....

??? ?

FINDING THE RIGHT THING TO WEAR

UNEXPECTED PERIOD

BUYING CONDOMS DISCREETLY

ASSAULT COURSE

OF BEING A GIRL

PART ONE

REACHING HIGH SHELVES IN SUPERMARKETS

BEING TOLD TO SMILE

OPENING JAM JARS

DANCING WITHOUT GETTING CREEPY LOOKS...

THE FEMALE

THE EVERYDAY CHALLENGE

BEING ONE
OF "THE GUYS"

BEING
HEARD

NATURE
WEES

UNREALISTIC
EXPECTATIONS

THE SEVEN

Social

LUST

CREEPILY STALKING THAT GUY YOU'VE NEVER MET AND USING HIS PHOTO AS YOUR SCREENSAVER, PRETENDING HE'S YOUR BOYFRIEND.

GLUTTONY

ALLOWING YOURSELF TO BE BRAINWASHED BY POP-UP ADS AND ORDERING JUNK FOOD WITHOUT EVEN KNOWING IT.

GREED

ADDING FAR MORE PEOPLE AS FRIENDS THAN YOU'LL EVER NEED; WHO SAYS YOU HAVE TO INTERACT WITH THEM?!!

SLOTH

WATCHING EVERY POSSIBLE RELATED VIDEO AUTOMATICALLY PLAY OUT RATHER THAN GETTING UP OFF YOUR ARSE TO STOP IT.

DEADLY SINS

Media

WRATH

CYBER-STALKING YOUR EX... THEN HIS EX... FOLLOWED BY HER EX... AND MAYBE HIS EX... AND EVERYONE ELSE THAT YOU HATE AND WANT TO PUSH OVER.

ENVY

OBSESSIVELY MONITORING THAT ANNOYING GIRL'S NUMBER OF FOLLOWERS AND REFRESHING YOUR OWN PAGE EVERY SEVEN SECONDS IN THE HOPE OF GAINING MORE THAN HER.

PRIDE

CONTINUOUSLY USING UP ALL THE MEMORY ON YOUR PHONE BY TAKING SELFIES AND EXPERIMENTING WITH THE MOST TRANSFORMATIVE FILTERS AND CROPPING OPTIONS.

nice and
personal

**"HEY YOU ;) HAD
NOT UP TO MUCH
OUT IN ABIT. HO**

Vague...

typo...

suggests a lack of
editing/thought
before sending

LAZY
GRAMMAR

OF TEXTING

BEHIND THE MESSAGE?

een?
cheeky?
flirty?

indifferent?

N ALRIGHT DAY.
NOW, MIGHT GO
BOUT YOU XX"

MORE THAN ONE KISS
= MORE THAN JUST FRIENDS?

No question mark
— do you want
to know or not?!

Why do i...

...CARE SO MUCH?

... HAVE FRENEMIES?

...OWN SO MANY SHOES?

...GO TO THE TOILET IN PAIRS?

... TRY TO LOOK LIKE OTHER GIRLS?

... LOVE FAIRY LIGHTS?

What I Say → What I Mean

YOU'VE EATEN ENOUGH → LET ME HAVE IT INSTEAD

YOUR HAIR LOOKS SOOO NICE LIKE THAT → DON'T YOU DARE CUT IT

I'M JUST GONNA JUMP INTO THE BATHROOM → SEE YOU IN APPROX. 2½ HOURS

DID YOU FINISH THE CHOCOLATE? → YOU'D BETTER START RUNNING...

DOES THIS LOOK ALRIGHT? → THERE IS ONLY ONE ANSWER

ARE YOU ASLEEP? → DO YOU WANT SEX?

IT DOESN'T MATTER... — BUT IT REALLY DOES...

GIRL APPROVED

The #1 Bestseller

PRO CRASTINATE™

AVOID RESPONSIBILITIES LIKE A CHAMP!*

* WARNING: THIS PRODUCT MAY CAUSE SEVERE LACK OF ACHIEVEMENT

i GOT NOTHING DONE TODAY ... AND i FEEL GREAT !

APATHY iS NOTHING TO BE ASHAMED OF

PRO-CRASTINATE™ HAS HELPED ME SO MUCH TO DO NOTHING

i REALLY SHOULD GET ROUND TO TRYING OUT THIS PRODUCT...

i CAN'T GET ENOUGH

WHAT I WISH I WORE

SASSY SIDE BUN

A NATURAL AIR OF CONFIDENCE

DESIGNER SHIRT

IMMACULATE NAILS

POWER SUIT (WITH SEVERE SHOULDERS)

COCKY STANCE

FANCY LEATHER CLUTCH

CUNNING HEELS

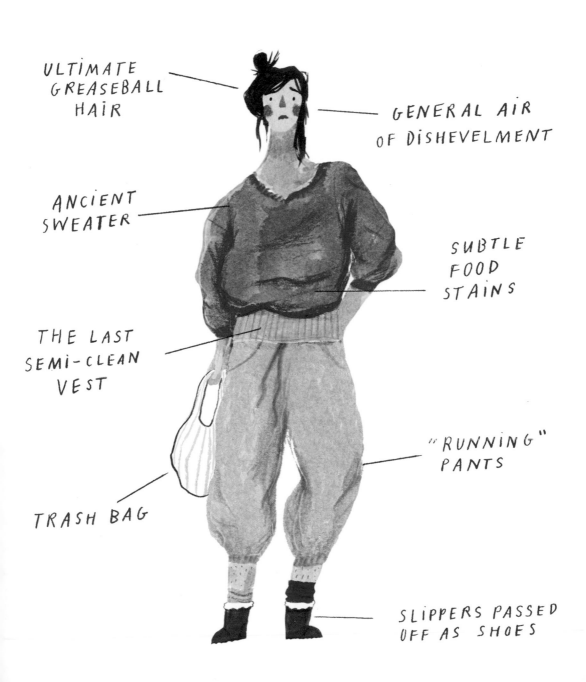

WHAT i WISH i BOUGHT

FRESH FLOWERS

FLIGHTS TO
FARAWAY
LANDS

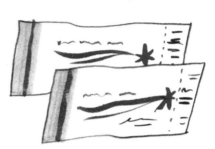

EXTRAVAGANT
FACE CREAM

DESIGNER JEWELLERY

EXPENSIVE
MAKE-UP

PHILOSOPHICAL
BOOKS

WHAT i ACTUALLY BOUGHT

CHEAP CHOCOLATE

SANITARY PRODUCTS

PAINKILLERS

TRASHY MAGS

ECONOMY TOILET PAPER

TRAGIC SANDWICH

CONQUERED THE WORLD

SPOKE TO EVERY RELATIVE OF MINE

DANCED IN A FOUNTAIN

HAD COFFEE WITH MY BEST FRIEND

WHAT I ACTUALLY DID

SPENT 2 ½ HOURS CYBER-STALKING
FRIENDS OF FRIENDS OF FRIENDS...

ENDLESS STREAMING BINGE

TOOK 45
(UNUSABLE) SELFIES

COUNTED THE LIKES
ON EVERY ONE OF
MY PROFILE PICTURES

SHAMELESSLY GORGED

CHAPTER 5

How to be a better girl

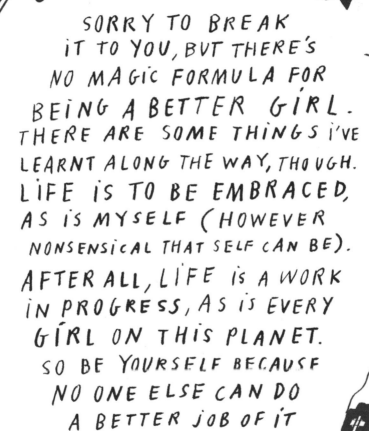

SORRY TO BREAK
IT TO YOU, BUT THERE'S
NO MAGIC FORMULA FOR
BEING A BETTER GIRL.
THERE ARE SOME THINGS I'VE
LEARNT ALONG THE WAY, THOUGH.
LIFE IS TO BE EMBRACED,
AS IS MYSELF (HOWEVER
NONSENSICAL THAT SELF CAN BE).
AFTER ALL, LIFE IS A WORK
IN PROGRESS, AS IS EVERY
GIRL ON THIS PLANET.
SO BE YOURSELF BECAUSE
NO ONE ELSE CAN DO
A BETTER JOB OF IT
THAN YOU.

NEW ME

* Read more biographies

* INVEST IN MYSELF MORE

* BE ABLE TO RUN GRACEFULLY

* Understand my private parts

* WATCH LESS CRAP

* STOP CARING ABOUT WHAT OTHER PEOPLE THINK

* COOK MORE

(LEARN)

RESOLUTIONS

* MAKE MORE TIME FOR THE RIGHT PEOPLE

* MAKE LESS TIME FOR THE WRONG PEOPLE

* Give myself more of a break?

* LEARN ANOTHER LANGUAGE

* EXERCISE EVERYDAY

* Be more generous

* STOP WRITING LISTS...

LET'S GET

PHYSICAL

my BUCKET LIST

FACE MY FEARS

CROWD SURF

CLIMB A MOUNTAIN

REACH TOTAL HAPPINESS

Go bareback horseriding

DO THE SPLITS (BOTH WAYS)

Run a marathon

BUY A COFFEE FOR A STRANGER

join a FLASH MOB

STREAK at a GAME

LEARN SIGN LANGUAGE

VISIT ALL 7 CONTINENTS

SEE A COMET

learn yoga

JUMP OUT OF A PLANE (PREFERABLY WITH A PARACHUTE)

BECOME A monKey WHISPERER

OWN A DOG

WIN AN AWARD

SEE THE WORLD

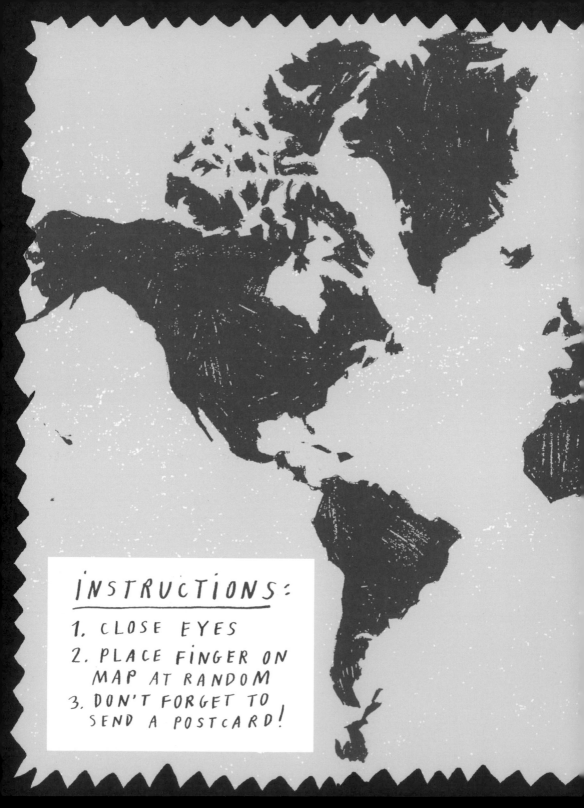

INSTRUCTIONS:

1. CLOSE EYES
2. PLACE FINGER ON MAP AT RANDOM
3. DON'T FORGET TO SEND A POSTCARD!

```
C N i D T S H E C A Q A R Y M R B K
B A R E E R A C W S F M X A Z L Y B
E M Y D J O M G i A H V L N G O D T
L C O K N P X V M M T P O W D V C R
H G J N E F U i O Q U T Q U F E Z E
Y F Q R E i L D P O R Y V W X B D A
B Z C J M Y S T N S S R X Y A C Z S
T D N L R i S M B E A U T Y G O P U
X O U A W K L Z A C R W j K N O E R
Y W A V Z L K D N A B S U H O F L E
F B P Q C j B M O R i B H L G M V W
H G A L L i V P N E H N E i R F L H
E E R D i L A Z i E A C S D U R O X
G C T F D Q C j O R C R F i T E O L
J H N i K U A N i P H E C A E P W A
R M E L S K T M G Q i F O G i V R 6
V H R T U A i Y X H L E H T H E Y E
S T S R T K O N L Z D S U C C E S S
O L N Q A X N K K F R E E D O M G T
T A U O T T S O i E E H C E R T S O
V E P H S W E A V j N T V E O A S
O W U A L A M O W O F i G E M i T O
i C S R E D L T Y A W i S S E M E
G F R i E N D S H i P R M E L E O N
R E G H P E i L F E i A G H E C R V
```

I should learn to
Embrace
MYSELF

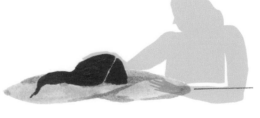

#COOLEST

IN H

GiRL GANG

VOTES FOR WOMEN

TORY ———————————

ADVICE FROM MY FUTURE SELF

"SLOW DOWN – NOT EVERYTHING NEEDS TO HAPPEN AT ONCE.

DON'T BE A DICK. BEING NICE PAYS OFF.

LIVE IN THE PRESENT – DON'T FUSS OVER WHAT MIGHT NEVER HAPPEN.

SHUT UP. YOU LOOK GREAT.

YOU DON'T NEED TO TRY SO HARD WITH PEOPLE; THEY'RE JUST AS WRAPPED UP IN THEMSELVES AS YOU ARE.

MAKE THE TIME AND EFFORT FOR THOSE WHO TRULY MATTER. NOW.

DEFINE YOURSELF BY WHAT YOU DO NOT WHAT YOU HAVE."

---

* I'M SURE THERE WAS MORE BUT I GOT TOO DISTRACTED BY HOW LOW MY BOOBS ARE GOING TO GET....

MY PEARLS OF WISDOM
I'VE GATHERED ALONG THE WAY

HALF OF INSPIRATION IS BEING BUSY

she saw herself as a work in progress

WORRYING IS A WASTE OF CREATIVE ENERGY

YOU CAN'T BE ALL THINGS TO ALL PEOPLE

NO ONE HAS EVER BECOME POOR BY GIVING

the people that matter don't mind. The people that mind don't matter.

TODAY WE'RE THE YOUNGEST WE'RE EVER GOING TO BE

Change only comes from great PAIN or great LOVE

PERHAPS WHEN YOU FORGET YOURSELF is WHEN YOU'RE MOST LIKELY TO BE REMEMBERED

BE PRESENT ALWAYS

Happiness isn't about getting what you want — it's about appreciating what you already have

NEVER JUDGE YOUR INSIDES BY SOMEONE'S OUTSIDES

LIFE is something to EXPLORE and EXPERIENCE first hand *

THE GIRL

ARM WING
A HYBRID OF AN ARM AND A WING
(I.E. EXCESS FLAB)

BLING
SHINY, OFTEN NON-EXPENSIVE-BUT-TRYING-TO-LOOK-IT
JEWELLERY

CHANGING ROOM DOOM
THE COMMON TRAUMA SUFFERED BY TRYING
ON CLOTHES IN A PUBLIC ESTABLISHMENT

CRY-AGRAM
A DIAGRAM OF PRE-CRYING SYMPTOMS

CYBER-STALKING
THE ACT OF VIRTUALLY PREYING UPON AN OBLIVIOUS
INDIVIDUAL WHO HAS NO IDEA OF THE HOURS SPENT
SCRUTINISING THEIR ONLINE PROFILE

GLOSSARY

DANCEABILITY
PRACTICALITY OF A GARMENT

DE-SEXIFICATION
THE ABILITY TO INSTANTLY COUNTERACT ANY PORTRAYAL OF SEXINESS IN ONE'S APPEARANCE (SHOULD THE OCCASION CALL FOR IT)

FRENEMY
A PERSON WITH WHOM ONE APPEARS TO BE FRIENDLY DESPITE AN UNDERLYING DISLIKE OR RIVALRY

GRANNY PANTIES
SUPER HIGH-WAIST, BAGGY, BUM-SWALLOWING KNICKERS WORN BY GIRLS WHO ENJOY COMFORT, WHATEVER THE COST

GREASEBALL
EXCESSIVELY GREASY HAIR

HORMONAL
A DANGEROUS AND ACCUSATORY TERM USED AGAINST A WOMAN WHO EXPRESSES ANY FORM OF EMOTION

HYGIENE CRIMES
BAD DOMESTIC HABITS THAT SHOULD BE ILLEGAL

THE GIRL

"I WOKE UP LIKE THIS"

A DELUSIONAL TERM USED TO SUGGEST NATURAL PERFECTION

LBD LITTLE BLACK DRESS (THANKS, COCO)

MOM JEANS

TYPICALLY HIGH-WAISTED, BAGGY-ISH
JEANS DESIGNED FOR COMFORT

MOODSWINGS & ROUNDABOUTS

THE EMOTIONAL PLAYGROUND THAT IS A GIRL'S LIFE

NAGOMETER

A SCALE USED TO MEASURE HOW NAGGY A PERSON IS

NATURE WEE

THE AWKWARD TASK OF URINATING OUTDOORS

NEW ME RESOLUTIONS

AN ALTERNATIVE SELF-IMPROVEMENT PLAN TIMED TO
THE NEEDS OF THE INDIVIDUAL RATHER THAN A NEW YEAR

GLOSSARY

NIGHT OUT-FIT
ATTIRE FOR EVENING LEISURE ACTIVITIES

#NOFILTER
AN HONEST PORTRAYAL OF AN UNEDITED SUBJECT

SELFIE
THE SHAMELESS, NARCISSISTIC ACT OF PHOTOGRAPHING ONESELF

SHIT-TINTED GLASSES
OPP. ROSE-TINTED GLASSES

SPILLAGE
THE LEAKAGE OF BOOB, BUM OR ANY OTHER BODY PART STRUGGLING TO BE CONTAINED WITHIN AN ITEM OF CLOTHING

"SPORTSWEAR"
PRACTICAL ATTIRE TO SUGGEST AN ACTIVE LIFESTYLE (OFTEN DECEPTIVE)

VOM
THE UNPLEASANT ACT OF REGURGITATION

RIGHT.
i SHOULD
PROBABLY GET
DRESSED...

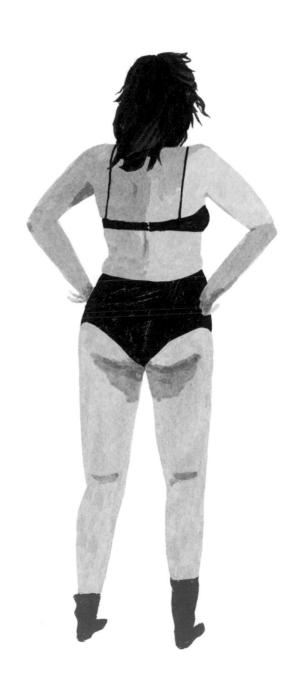

THANKS

♡

TO THE AMAZING GIRLS i KNOW,
HAVE KNOWN AND AM YET TO KNOW.

THE HASTINGS CLAN, KINGSTON
CREW, MY SOUTHSEA SISTERS,
REIGATE LADS, TWINKLE AND
LONDON BABES. YOU ALL KNOW
WHO YOU ARE, YOU BEAUTIES!

i WOULD LIKE TO, AS ALWAYS,
THANK MY FAMILY AND THE
EVER-WONDERFUL ALISON XX